THE KIDS'
POCKET GUIDE
TO THE WORLD

Dear Camilla

May your life
be a great
journey around
the world

Simon

About the author

Simona Paravani-Mellinghoff is a proud godmother and a world traveller for work and for passion. Simona is Italian by birth, German by marriage and a world-citizen by nature. She combines a full-time job in financial services with various activities to support NGOs. This book is inspired by the many great girls and women she has met in her journeys, all wonderful examples of how passions and dreams can change lives and the world around us!

THE KIDS' POCKET GUIDE TO THE WORLD

By Simona Paravani-Mellinghoff

BROWN
DOG
BOOKS

Published under licence by Brown Dog Books and
The Self Publishing Partnership
7 Green Park Station, Bath BA1 1JB

www.selfpublishingpartnership.co.uk

ISBN printed book: 978-1-78545-032-7
ISBN e-book: 978-1-78545-033-4

Cover design by Kevin Rylands

Printed and bound by CPI Group (UK) Ltd, Croydon CR0 4YY

Dedication

This book is dedicated to my godchildren and their friends who will inherit this fantastic world of seven billion people. I hope it will help them to show us grown-ups why an open globalized world is a sea of opportunities, not a storm to shelter from.

To my wonderful husband Michael who every day gives me the courage, passion and hope to continue pursuing my dreams!

Introduction for the grown-ups

A globalised interconnected world is no choice: cheaper travel, innovative technologies and human curiosity are driving all seven billion of us ever closer...

Our everyday life is a testament to how interconnected and global we have become: we can order the same Starbucks *latte* in Beijing's Forbidden City or next to the London Eye; via social networks like Facebook, we often know more about our virtual neighbours in other countries than the people actually living next door to us.

A globalised interconnected world is no choice; however, we can decide whether to see it as a threat or as an opportunity... This booklet sides unequivocally and unashamedly with the latter option! Why? The world faces great challenges: there are more of us, we live longer, we consume more and we are needed less and less to produce the goods and services we want. Such challenges are truly global; know no boundaries; no frontiers. We most definitely have a better chance to overcome such challenges if we can count on the brains, hopes and dreams of seven billion people rather than just a handful!

To my godchildren and their friends who will inherit the planet

Dearest godchildren,
Your parents sure had a great sense of humour when they called me godmother: I regularly forget your birthdays, Christmas and various holidays, busy in some far-off corner of the world doing something completely incomprehensible to you and to 99 per cent of the rest of the population.

It certainly won't be me that teaches you to ride a bike or drive a car: your godmother is totally incompetent in all those important day-to-day things: when our Lord handed out these qualities, I simply wasn't around!

The only thing I can give you is this booklet, your personalised pocket guide to this wonderful complicated world, so that you feel at home wherever you go and see the world and its great changes as a sea of opportunities rather than as a storm to shelter from.

The Clouds of Hope

I met Mwangaza at a boarding school in Nairobi. There she was called Hope, it was easier in such a British institution, but to her family she was born Mwangaza, a Swahili name that means "she who brings light", and meeting her certainly illuminated me.

Even when she was little more than a child, she already had the wisdom of one who had lived at least seven lives; and to her belongs that memorable phrase that I love so much to repeat to those people spoilt by life and who don't know how lucky they are: "I don't consider myself poor, because I am rich in mind".

And, that Mwangaza was poor in the material sense of the word, there is very little doubt. The definition of poor according to the United Nations is a person who lives on less than one dollar a day, or less than the price of a pencil. Mwangaza's family were really poor: mother, father and seven children, who lived in a village on the plateaus of Kenya; the most precious thing they had was two goats, whose milk could be exchanged for other essential goods, meat and sometimes luxuries like exercise books for school or shoes.

You have to understand that in rural Africa the majority of

9

the population don't receive a salary like your mum and dad do when they work. Theirs is an economy often still based on bartering: milk for wheat, meat for milk.

There is little money around and schooling costs money. For instance, teachers have to be paid and books bought. So for Mwangaza and her brother, school was a luxury they could only afford from time to time. In times of feast all seven siblings, including Mwangaza, attended school. In times of famine everyone stayed at home; in the *so-so* times, the boys went and the girls stayed at home to work and collect water.

Mwangaza liked school, especially mathematics and geography (take note, dear godchildren!). When the teacher told her of far-off places, pointing them out on an old globe which must had been at least forty years old, Mwangaza dreamt of being an airline pilot.

I think the idea of being able to move without having to walk had a special fascination for Mwangaza, who regularly walked the equivalent of a small marathon to get to school or collect water. In rural Africa, it is not at all unusual for children to walk for two or three hours per day to fetch and carry water, for domestic use and for the animals, as well as long distances to and from school. They walk immense stretches of land, often alone, in an unforgiving hot and hostile environment.

Mwangaza was right in the middle of those stretches of land, at the well, on the day when heaven brought gloom down on her house and Evil knocked at the door. It was a faceless Evil that in Africa kills and has orphaned millions of children; an Evil so terrifying that in parts of Africa they are even afraid to talk about it and so, in the silence, it kills even more remorselessly.

The Evil was already in the frail body of Mwangaza's mum and every day it took away a little light from her eyes and life from her sweet smile.

The Clouds of Hope

For Mwangaza, the Evil meant the end of school, the end of playing hide-and-seek with the other village children. Mwangaza was 10 years old and she was the eldest sister. There was a house to tend to as well as her little brothers – babes in arms. Her mum was used to stroking her hair that was so short, frizzy and rebellious. Now it was Mwangaza who had to remove the tufts of hair that the Evil tore regularly from the head of her frail mother.

From the day the Evil had knocked on their door, the other members of the village avoided Mwangaza's house, fearing, out of ignorance, that the Evil would transmit itself to them by breathing the same air, by sitting on the same pavement, or perhaps by looking into the eyes of the one whom the Evil had already visited. So the Evil and, above all, cruel ignorance forced Mwangaza to live as an outcast in their humble little house.

In her days of isolation, Mwangaza often looked up into that sky so blue that she'd wanted to fly over as a pilot and the clouds soon became her playmates. She dreamt of leaping from one cloud to the next. She asked herself what on earth could be hidden in the clouds. She imagined that under that fluffy white sheet lurked cascades of chocolate, giant see-saws and a world that the Evil could not reach. This, thought Mwangaza, was the place where her mum would go when her suffering ended and where Mwangaza and her siblings would meet their mother again one day.

In those long days of waiting without meaning and without end, Mwangaza had baptised each cloud in the sky. There was *little loaf*: the small chubby cloud that must be all full of sweet things, Mwangaza imagined. Then there were the *heavenly step-sisters*: these were the big black clouds that were the first to arrive announcing the rains. Then there were those *magic dust*: customarily small and light, that seemed to disappear and reappear as if by magic.

Mwangaza and the clouds had been friends for some time when one day there came to the village men with machetes who, with senseless hate in their minds, began to ransack the village and set the homes on fire leaving families homeless and lives swept away like leaves in the wind.

Then the cloud friends, who saw everything from above, decided to help their dear Mwangaza and all together made it black as night and tipped water on the village like a waterfall. Mwangaza's mum told her to run away as fast as she could. So after a last kiss to her sweet mother, Mwangaza ran away like lightning concealed by the darkness of the sky that her friends-the clouds- extended over her like a protective mantel.

Days came and went before Mwangaza reached safety. On the way she met other families fleeing from the men with machetes and together they crossed the immense plateaus until one day they arrived at the big city, Nairobi.

At school, Mwangaza had seen pictures of Nairobi; but was not prepared for how big it was, and how many people lived there.

In fact, Nairobi is a megalopolis with more than three million inhabitants and where the most expensive modern cars share the road with cows and donkeys: the roads are chaotic and motorists often experience long traffic jams. There seem to be no rules, but the traffic still moves somehow and sooner or later you arrive at your chosen destination.

The houses were so tall that Mwangaza could hardly see her cloud friends and there were endless lights and those advertising billboards, so big and beautiful, that promised a life of comfort and wealth. The most beautiful African women in elegant dresses and flashy jewellery posing in front of various, usually non-essential, items.

One of the women she met on the way offered to put up Mwangaza with her relatives in the Eastlands: a shanty town mostly without light and running water, so typical of the poorest areas of African megalopolises (and not only African!).

Mwangaza found herself in a shack already overcrowded with women, other children and men coming and going. They appeared often drunk and often violent. There was shack after shack, one attached to another, all theatres of the same stories. Generations of women: daughters, mothers, grandmothers, trapped in domestic servitude by the thought that there was no other way to live. Their lives revolved around the shack and its walls served as a prison as they tended day after day to the needs of such violent men. Moments of kindness were matched by periods of harsh brutality.

Mwangaza was little more than a child. She had studied the globe; she had seen the photos of the women pilots who criss-crossed the skies indomitably. She had known the freedom of running on the plateaus with the clouds as travelling companions. She knew in her heart that there was another way of life, a way far from those shacks, from those chains that were invisible yet weighed so heavily on her.

So one day when a stupid bully tried to be disrespectful to her, Mwangaza said no, leaving the bully in question with a nice second-degree burn on his........to remind him (forever, you hope) that you don't lay a finger on a woman and especially a girl at that. Putting down the bully, Mwangaza knew she had only one option: escape, and so, in bare feet, as when she was up there on the plateaus, she ran without stopping. As she looked up towards the sky, the city dust, dazzling lights and its polluted heat made it hard for her to see the stars or her friends – the clouds

She spent days living on the road, feeding off refuse – mainly vegetables left behind in the evening on the stalls of the open markets. She slept mostly by day. It was safer because the comings and goings of the city warded off the attacks of troublemakers. At night, like a stray dog, she would roam the city in search of food.

Out on her search for food one night Mwangaza, by chance, came across an imposing building with a strange smell of incense coming out of it. Poking her head through a half-opened window, Mwangaza noticed a lady, dressed all in white, standing at the front of the building putting out a large number of candles. Mwangaza entered the building and hid herself behind the chairs at the back. But the woman in white was alert and noticed the tiny figure at the back of the church and recognised the fear and hunger in Mwangaza's eyes. "Come, little one," she said with her smooth melodic voice in a language. Mwangaza wasn't familiar with.

The lady in white was called Sister Luisa and she came from a far-off country with many mountains and snow. Without asking questions, Sister Luisa gave bread and tea to poor Mwangaza and built a bunk bed there in a corner of the kitchen.

For the first time in months Mwangaza slept peacefully that night. Our heroine had happened upon a Carmelite convent – an order of Catholic nuns founded in the sixteenth century to help the poor and other unfortunate people.

Unfortunately, however, the convent did not have an orphanage and was not equipped to care for children. This significant detail certainly did not discourage Sister Luisa, whose only rule was that there should be no rules that could prevent anyone from doing the right charitable thing. The determined sister therefore decided, with the complicity of several other sisters and unknown to the mother superior, to take care of little Mwangaza. They prepared her a little room in the basement, windowless, but at least there she could sleep safely under blankets! One or two hot meals were also assured every day.

The Clouds of Hope

The company of the sprightly sisters helped to pass the day. Each of them told her stories of their native lands. And what places they were! From the Trentino Alps where Sister Luisa went to school on skis, ("Who knows what these skis are?" Mwangaza asked herself), to the pagodas of Thailand where Sister Mary was born. Although safe and well looked after by the pious fold, Mwangaza's eyes still showed sadness of being without her family. She missed the outside world, playing hide-and-seek with the other children, the open paths on the plateaus, and, above all, school.

One day she burst into tears in front of Sister Luisa, saying that she couldn't dream anymore; that from an early age, before the Evil knocked on the door of her house, she had wanted to be a pilot, but now if she tried to dream, the dream flew away quickly like birds scenting a hunt.

At these words Sister Luisa decided it was time to call for the help of the "higher levels", not so much divine ones who – we know – have unpredictable ways and means, but those literally on the higher levels of the convent. Time to ask help from Sister Albertina, known as Irma.

Although the diminutive "ina" might give the impression of a docile and submissive little nun, the mother superior, Sister Albertina was what you might call a man through and through under those monastic robes. She was shrouded in great mystery: some say she had been a great lady of high society, some even an international spy, before tying the knot with the Lord: but alas that part of the story is bound in the deepest mystery and not even your godmother knows about it.

One evening after Mass, Sister Luisa went to her, cup of tea in hand, with a slightly penitent look. "Dear Sister Irma," she began. "I've gone and done it again and I've taken, shall we say, l bit of a liberty with the rules." Sister Irma who, although rigorous in getting others to obey rules, had perhaps ignored one or two in her own life, welcomed the sister's confession with a benevolent smile.

Having listened to Mwangaza's story, she asked to see the girl. Mwangaza was a little intimidated by this minute figure with sharp feline eyes, but as we well know, Mwangaza certainly did not lack courage.

Mwangaza spoke to the mother superior about her family, of the Evil, of the men with machetes and of the troublemakers. Sister Irma, who had survived all of two world wars, knew all about armed men with bad intentions and saw a bit of herself in that spirited courageous girl. So she decided without hesitation that Mwangaza could stay with them safely in the convent. This resolved the immediate emergency, but the fundamental problem nevertheless remained – Mwangaza's education.

"Help her," thought Sister Irma. "Yes, but how?" It was clear to all the sisters that orphanages or state institutions could do little; so crowded were they that they would not have taken kindly to another mouth to feed, especially one, by local conventions, already old enough to work. And then no institution would have been able to satisfy her hunger for learning. They wanted to give her an education, but how?

Divine Providence, as we know, works in unexpected ways, and for Mwangaza it came through an advertising billboard for a well-known brand of trainers. Indeed, it was the period of the Olympics and the poster celebrated the renowned successes of Kenyan marathon runners. And so the athletic legs of that poster inspired Sister Irma, intent on her daily chores.

"Praise the Lord!" she exclaimed. She ran into the convent and gathered the sisters. "Sisters," she said, with that touch of pride of someone who knows a thing or two, "I've got the solution for Mwangaza. The girl can run, let's call these sports companies, tell them her story and ask them to help her to run towards her dreams."

The idea was welcomed with great enthusiasm, but monastic life does not prepare well for knowledge of sport, so the plan presented incredible practical challenges: "how can we identify potentially interested companies?"

And so Divine Providence took the determined sisters to a local internet café. We Europeans are often a bit ignorant and are used to thinking of Africa as technologically backward with communication systems of bongos and carrier pigeons. In reality, Africa, and Kenya in particular, is at the cutting edge of several technological sectors, especially those linked to the supply of internet and mobile phone services (for example, the Kenyans are leaders in the use of mobile phones for payments).

But let's go back to the sisters at the internet café and their search for sports companies with interests in girls who can run. Having made a suitable search and identified interested companies, they got the proverbial pens out and began contacting potential benefactors.

Given their renowned and remarkable employer, the sisters were careful not to waste time with half measures and wrote directly to top management.

Sometimes giving Divine Providence a helping hand doesn't do any harm, and so the sisters provided the letter with a lot of Vatican seals (i.e. a sort of certificate of authenticity issued by the Holy See) "borrowed" for the occasion: it shouldn't be done, according to the rules, but it was a good cause, after all, and so the sisters decided that one or two more stamps weren't really a sin, but rather poetic licence in the interpretation of canonical rules!

The letter reached an important lady – Lady X. Lady X lived in the United States and she was head of the ladies' sports division of the biggest company in the business. It took just a click of the fingers from the powerful Lady X and two athletic gentlemen arrived at the convent who, in the name of sport and good causes, wanted to see Mwangaza run.

What frenzy in the convent. What joy. God had heard their prayers. Naturally the sisters knew very little about sport and running; obviously Mwangaza could run long distances but were they long enough or fast enough for the gentlemen of sport?

Mwangaza was taken to a large stadium where statuesque-bodied young athletes stood out against the sky with powerful elegance. Next to them, Mwangaza looked like a poorly nourished cat next to a lion. With the sisters as cheerleaders, Mwangaza gave it her best: she ran long distances, short distances, jumping up, jumping down. But the gentlemen of sport, stopwatches in hand, didn't seem very impressed.

At the end of the day the gentlemen of sport wrote to Lady X and reported back that yes, the girl was gifted, but not enough to make her an Olympic champion and so it didn't seem in their interests to give financial support.

Poor Mwangaza, who knew she had given her all, was devastated to learn that even her best wasn't good enough for her to take flight. You could see in her eyes the sadness of one who suddenly felt imprisoned by her birth and the set of circumstances life had thrown at her in the short time on earth. She felt trapped in a black tunnel where the word "hope" never set foot.

Mother Superior Irma knew that, although faith and optimism are not always enough to realise your dreams, desperation and pessimism are always sufficient to realise nightmares. Therefore she didn't want Mwangaza to resign herself to the destiny of dying within herself, without having first lived.

So that evening, in what was almost a complete departure

for the convent, there was a party. Mother Superior Irma decided that every sister should cook a delicacy and there would be a banquet and thanks given to God for the good things on the table and the others He would give them in future.

Mwangaza had never experienced such exquisite and diverse food– food to make her lick her lips and make her smile at life once again. That night, with the flavours and tastes of the supper still in her mind, Mwangaza dreamt of her cloud friends and her mum who was now living with them in the giant plateaus and waterfalls of chocolate in the sky. In the dream her mum spoke to her saying, "Mwangaza, carry on flying."

While Mwangaza was dreaming like this, Lady X on the other side of the world was reading the reports of the gentlemen of sport. By luck or Divine Grace (depending on your point of view), Lady X was very clear that whoever pursued their dream was a good investment for her company, as much as, if not more than, whoever pursued Olympic glory: also because if it was only Olympians who bought trainers they would sell very few of them.

So it was that Lady X, in the name of dreams, wrote a big cheque to put Mwangaza on track and give her the education necessary to take off one day as a real pilot.

Thanks to that cheque, the doors of one of the best schools in Nairobi opened to Mwangaza, the College of St Mary's, where she could begin her education. She could thus run towards her dream of being a pilot.

And it was precisely at St Mary's that your godmother met Mwangaza for the first time. They had asked me to mentor several of their most promising students and, as often happens in these situations, it was the mentor who learned and the pupil who taught.

From then on I have followed my pupil-mentor's

development with interest and some years ago I received a photo of her in pilot's uniform. Have a little guess who her first and most enthusiastic passengers were? The Carmelite sisters with Mother Superior Irma at their head.

The Green Cinderellas

Imagine a deep -blue sea from which rise mountains that seem like giant *panettoni*. Add white beaches teeming with people running or playing volleyball.

Welcome to Rio de Janeiro, my dear godchildren, a city synonymous with beauty of all kinds, some of which you will appreciate better when you are a bit older!

In this city, known for its beauty, Helena was born, the princess of this story. She was a princess without a crown, because Brazil is not a monarchy, but blue blood and throne aside, she had all the credentials of a princess: a house like a castle, as many servants as she wanted, wonderful clothes and even a private plane to take her and her mum shopping in New York. Yes, because although Brazil is considered a poor country, it has its fair share of extremely rich people.

Brazil is a country of over 200 million people, over 20 per cent of whom live below the poverty line; in other words, nearly one in every five people you meet potentially has difficulty eating every day! In spite of enormous progress in recent years in terms of economic growth, average income per person is about 10,000 dollars a year, but that average hides people who are very, very, rich indeed and many who are not rich at all.

In fact, it is estimated that in Brazil the top 10 per cent of the population earns 40 dollars for each one dollar that the poorest 10 per cent earns. Our princess Helena sat comfortably in that fortunate percentage of the population. Indeed, Helena's life was a bit like being constantly in the fast lane of a motorway. You could call this the motorway of life where, if you are lucky, you can move freely, experience few challenges, and be surrounded by other fortunate types with the smile of the easy life stamped on their face.

Helena's future was mostly a foregone conclusion. She would marry a respectable prince, and she would be wealthy and hopefully happy in the fast lane of life up to her last breath. No need to work or worry how much money there is in the bank.

But we know, although life in the fast lane is normally easy and hilarious, even then it holds its surprises that are not always pleasant. One day Helena's mother and sister were coming back from a birthday party at the Country Club: a most sumptuous place with heated swimming pools, tennis courts to make Wimbledon envious and lawns mown to such perfection they looked as if a hairdresser had cut them.

It was already nightfall and it was raining cats and dogs as you only find in the tropical storms. The driver was going slowly on those slippery wet roads, but alas, bandits, like cowardly pirates, were hiding in the shadows of the evening roads to ambush the cars of the wealthy. The conscientious caution of the driver represented an opportunity for ambush. The driver was shot through the window and killed on the spot.

Against three petty criminals for whom the value of life, theirs included, was almost nothing, the driver didn't count for much, gunned down with a pistol. One more number for the terrible statistics of violence that, like the plague, torment the everyday life and conscience of the country. Indeed, Brazil has more than 20 homicides for every 100,000 people, and this is a much higher number than in countries like China or Japan where there is 1 homicide per 100,000 people.

The criminals then vented their anger on Helena's mum, guilty in their eyes of being beautiful and rich, hence a symbol of that life that they could only dream of with spiteful envy. The police arrived just in time to stop the pirates, poisoned with rage and drugs, turning on Helena's little sister. There were shots, shouts and, in the end, bodies on the pavement.

The fear, the senseless violence of that day of rain, took away from Helena's little sister the ability to speak. Even now, years after the tragic event, she lives barricaded in an impenetrable silence. It is as if her voice was stolen on that dreadful night but, in truth, she lost the will to communicate with a world that could be so cruel.

In our Princess Helena, then, that day of rain that such pain and mourning brought to her family created a visceral need to understand. So there began days, months, years, of difficult questions; why such hate, why that senseless violence and hatred for life? Were the walls of the fast lane of life perhaps so impenetrable as to take away all hope of a change of lane, for those not born there? A life without hope is, as we well know, fertile terrain for desperation, hate and all the other cancers of the human soul.

These questions gradually took our princess far away from her life and ever more into contact with the reality of the roads crowded with hopeless faces – the look worn every day by Sol, an Indio woman from Mexico City, tiny, with skin burnt by the sun and neglect.

She would have been about 40, but the wretched life had put at least another 15 years of fatigue and lack of care on her body and face. Sol was a "*basurera*" – she rummaged among the refuse to find something to sell: metal, bottles, various oddments.

Indeed, in many developing countries there are no organised refuse collections and recycling systems. No big smelly dustbin lorries, no multi-coloured waste bins or recycling facilities. Consequently, it is estimated that 50 to 100 per cent of refuse collection is left to these ecological "do-it-yourself" operatives who rummage through the noxious waste, without any protection, in search of objects to sell. This negatively impacts on their health and well-being. It is a dangerous job that often causes these unfortunates to contract diseases that they have no money to cure. Indeed, in a metropolis like Mexico City where it is thought there are 15,000 "do-it-yourself" refuse collectors, the average lifespan of these informal ecological operatives is between 40 and 50 years; this means a good 20 years shorter than the broader population's: 20 fewer Christmases, more than 7000 fewer days to enjoy the company of those you love...

But let's go back to Sol, our Cinderella of the tip, and to Helena, the Princess of Rio de Janeiro, and to the strange coincidences of fate that brought them to meet.

Helena was in Mexico City working for free for a programme using volunteers to teach the use of computers to children in the most deprived schools. She had just finished her shift and, with another volunteer, was standing in front of the rusty gates of the school complaining about the day, unenthusiastic colleagues, in short, the world and everything else.

Just then the two were interrupted in their daily grumblings by shouts from Sol, who was being pestered by hoodies armed with spiked sticks, chasing her, and yelling "filthy beggar". Helena and the other volunteer rushed to help the tiny Sol, who had fallen to the floor. Helena made a human shield with her body while the other volunteer, a big young American boy, chased the hoodies away.

The Green Cinderellas

What a contrast, the image of Sol in the arms of the princess: Helena, with her long black hair, golden skin and model figure, was beautiful and elegant even in jeans. In contrast, poor Sol had on clothes for which such a definition would be generous. The word "rags" is more appropriate to describe Sol's clothing. Helena's golden skin was kissed with the sweet smell of expensive Chanel perfume, whereas Sol's had not seen water in days and smelt of a perfume called *dump stench*. Absolutely not recommended if you want to make a good first impression (think about your feet, at the end of the day, and multiply that fine perfume by a thousand!).

Helena gave Sol water and some rather crushed biscuits that she had in her rucksack. Sol, not used to being treated with such generosity, still less by strangers, burst into floods of tears, held back for goodness knows how long. Maybe it was the profundity and sincerity of that outburst; maybe Sol had something maternal in that embrace of hers, but the princess too gave in to tears held back for a long time – too long.

So Cinderella and the princess stayed there on the pavement of that dilapidated road consoling each other until late into the night. Those roads are not safe at that hour and certainly no taxis pass. Sol urged Helena to hide in her little house. Just a box of wood and mud that Sol shared with her mother, two sisters and her adolescent daughter Ximena.

On the walls there were photos and newspaper cuttings that Sol had found among the rubbish and Ximena called "pictures". With a certain pride, Ximena immediately pointed out that, in their house, they even had the Mona Lisa! This was a creased cutting of a mineral water advertisement that used the iconic image by Leonardo da Vinci, to which was added a fine glass of water with the label on full show.

Seeing Ximena's admiration for that banal

commercialisation of a masterpiece, Helena, smiling, confirmed that it was exactly the same as the original that she had seen in Paris, in fact almost better!

Sol told Helena that as well as her, her mother and her sisters were all "*basureras*", but hoped for a better future for Ximena, the first in their family to be able to go to school, thanks to their work as ecological operatives and to one of their sisters, Leandra, who worked as a home help in Europe and sent money from time to time.

The door of the house was always open and in the evening there was the coming and going of other "*basureras*": young, old and some who seemed ageless. Their faces all told the same story of struggle, disease and lack of education. Nevertheless, even under the heavy rags of misery, the common problems of all the women of the world were hiding; so the princess and the Cinderellas spent evenings talking or rather complaining about men and failed loves – those faded and those still to come.

So Helena met Dolores, the most eminent "*basurera*" of the group; the beautiful shapely lady who turned the heads of even the saints and finally the very religious Gimena, who said an Ave Maria of thanks for every tin she collected.

That evening saw the start of a friendship that was unusual in its members as much as in its consequences. Seeing as Princess Helena came from a family of business people and had a head for numbers, it didn't take much to understand that the Cinderellas, without realising it, were sitting on a gold mine: the combination of the rising cost of raw materials like metals, and the pressure to reduce waste in western countries, had indeed transformed so-called garbage into a real profit-making business potential. Straight away Helena convinced her "*basurera*" friends to form a company that they rightly called "Green Cinderellas", to give training and work to the local "*basureras*" in the area of recycling of glass and metal from collection to dispatch, satisfying the demands of specialised clients in the USA and Canada.

In fact the Green Cinderellas did not just limit themselves to the lowest paid and most noxious segment of the business, but carved themselves out a niche in the most lucrative part of the rubbish gold mine. Naturally, to set up a business, any business, takes quite a lot of money, so Princess Helena called in the men in grey suits whose job it was to manage her wealth.

The meeting took place in the lobby of a luxury hotel in Mexico City where Princess Helena arrived in an Armani suit and her business colleagues in clothes borrowed from the local charity shop. The men in grey suits were busy in their profound conversations about football and golf clubs when the novice entrepreneurs came into the red velvet lobby.

At the sight of the unusual union of princess-Cinderellas, there was an embarrassed silence in the hall until the smartest of the group remembered who was paying him and exchanged the necessary pleasantries with Helena and her colleagues. In the style of a true business consultant, Helena, our princess, began to articulate, figures in hand, why she wanted to invest 50 per cent of her assets in the Green Cinderellas. At the end of the presentation Helena concluded by giving the bewildered men the details of her bank account in which to deposit the capital.

The men in grey suits were flabbergasted. They thought they had been called to sanction a larger annuity or the purchase of a loft in Tribeca in New York. Even if they didn't dare open their mouths you could read in their faces what was going on in their minds. "Rubbish business, what kind of business proposal is that!"

Recovering from the initial shock, the men in grey suits began to make rather banal comments on the difficulties of running a business, on the costs of liquidating capital, etc.,

etc.: nothing that Helena could not respond to in kind.

After at least an hour of useless conversation our princess intervened and spoke first directly to the boss of the men in grey. Mr C – a middle-aged Englishman – is fondly called "Mr C" due to his love for cricket.

"My dear Helena," he began with his polished Eton accent and posh demeanour. "I understand your youthful enthusiasm. The stories of these unfortunates are so moving and so it is easy to influence a good soul like yours, but we have your future at heart. I am speaking to you as if you were my daughter. Do something else; you are a pretty girl, have fun, enjoy life, travel the world and maybe you will find a nice husband." And with that word "husband" he paused with the smile of one who has uttered a great truth.

Then he picked up the arrogant sermon again. "These are poor creatures and in part they deserve the Destiny that God has reserved for them. Let's give them a fine charitable donation, but let's leave them be. You, Miss Helena, are of another stripe; you belong to another world."

Helena, who had a fine Latin temperament, restrained herself from throwing something onto his empty head (entirely justifiable in such circumstance even if I normally abhor violence). With an almost murderous calm she replied, "My dear Mr C, I am very fortunate in life, not least because I am not your daughter, but I am the person to whom you owe your salary. If I remember rightly you are a great cricket fan, correct?"

Mr C nodded. "Good," Helena went on. "As there's no room in my businesses for paternalistic prisoners of prejudice, I am happy to tell you that with immediate effect you will have a lot more time to dedicate yourself to your favourite pastime: you're sacked."

The princess accompanied the word "sacked" with an elegant hand gesture that unhesitatingly indicated the door.

The Green Cinderellas

Mr C, bewildered, looked around him for the support of the other men in grey, but found none, and, humiliated, left the room for the oblivion he deserved.

Unfortunately there are still many Mr Cs in high places, but thankfully they are a dying species. One day, when you are grown up, dear godchildren, I hope you will see the Mr Cs of this world in the place that suits them best, an anthropological museum next to the troglodytes (and let's hope troglodytes are not too offended!).

The other men in grey, who didn't want to share the fate of Mr C, signed the cheque straight away and with that the Green Cinderellas were born.

The rest, as they say, is history. Today Green Cinderellas is one of the biggest companies in its sector in Latin America and its original members don't get their clothes from charity shops any more or live in wooden shacks, quite the opposite! Green Cinderellas continues to maintain a rigorous policy of training and education for its staff and their daughters.

And talking of daughters, Ximena, Sol's pride, became a high flyer and confirmed herself as the pride of the "*basureras*": after distinguishing herself at the prestigious American Harvard University, she was taken on by a leading sporting goods company and now, so well-informed sources tell me, she is head of the women's division. Partly because of her name and partly out of respect, everyone calls her Lady X.

The Frog and the Flower

This leg of our world tour takes us to a city that your godmother knows well because it is there that I was born: Bologna. Bologna is a prosperous hard-working city in the north of Italy with less than half a million inhabitants and known internationally for its food and for having given birth to what is said to be the oldest university in the world.

And it is in this little city, rich and a little provincial, that the protagonists of our modern fable, Jasmina and Maria Vittoria, were brought up. Even if both were living in the same city, their lives seemed to belong to separate worlds.

Jasmina lived with her parents and her three sisters in the little room adjacent to the greengrocers that her family kept open 24 hours a day, seven days a week. That small but well-stocked shop with its neon lights resembled a 1970s refectory. In a side street, in the historic centre of Bologna, was Eldorado for Jasmine and her family. Their passport to a better life than the one they could have aspired to in Bangladesh.

The father had left a small village in the north of Bangladesh nearly twenty years earlier in search of a better life than the one he saw before him. Bangladesh is a country of more than

The Frog and the Flower

160 million inhabitants. It is a young country with an average age of just 24 years, where only half of the population can read and write and poverty shows itself in the record number of underweight children and the painfully high rate of infant mortality. In Bangladesh, almost 50 children for every 1000 die before the age of one, compared with just three in a country like Germany.

Jasmina's father arrived in Bologna after a long journey of humiliation and vexation, made bearable only by that vital drug called hope. And indeed Mohamed's optimism had paid off. A legal immigrant, in a country where many of his compatriots are "invisible and without rights", he had been able to set up a business to put food on the family table and give his daughters the chance of a real education. In the humble abode, in spite of the limited space and second-hand furniture, there was, then, an air of hope, a dream of a better tomorrow.

There was only a five minute walk separating the homes of Jasmina and Maria Vittoria, but also 300 years of privilege. Maria Vittoria lived in a sixteenth century building with beautiful frescoes on the ceilings and crystal chandeliers worthy of the Palace of Versailles.

Years before Maria Vittoria's family occupied the whole building: four floors of splendour and breath-taking courtyards; but even the most enormous fortunes, if badly managed, come to a sticky end. And so "hard times" – you could say – had arrived even for Maria Vittoria's family, now forced to live on a "modest" floor of just 200 metres. Considering that the family consisted only of Maria Vittoria, her parents and their Mexican home help, they were hardly cramped! But as they say all things are relative and Maria Vittoria's family dared to count themselves almost unfortunate!

For a long time the only link between the world of Maria

Vittoria and that of Jasmina was Leandra, the Mexican home help who went to buy fruit and vegetables at Mohamed's shop and often stopped to chat with the girls and their mother. Leandra told them of Mexico and of her little niece Ximena, the first of the family to go to school, the pride of her family of "do-it-yourself ecological operatives"! From time to time Leandra would complain about her employers: "God," she said, "You gave them much, but you forgot to donate them the ability to appreciate their good fortune. They are poorer, in spirit, than the beggars in my country!"

Maria Vittoria's mum was almost ashamed to be able to afford just one home help and she had instructed Leandra to call herself a governess and not to reveal the details of their domestic set-up.

Maria Vittoria's mum looked at herself in the mirror, still pretty despite the years, but in her eyes was rooted an anger for having, she thought, wasted her beauty, marrying a small-time provincial lawyer. Although her husband came from an old aristocratic family, he was forced to let out what remained of his splendid home to continue living the high society lifestyle. "I was so pretty," she thought. "I should have aimed much higher!"

And with that anger in her eyes she looked at Maria Vittoria and swore to God that her daughter would not share the same fate. And so from her earliest days, Maria Vittoria was subject to a regime of rigorous exterior perfection. At 10 years old she already knew how to use eyebrow curlers like a true professional and by 12 she spent at least 30 minutes each morning doing her hair.

So a mixture of good genes, discreet means and incredible discipline saw to it that at 14, when youngsters usually seem like little frogs, Maria Vittoria was a true flower in the full flush of spring.

But as the frogs in fairy tales, if kissed, can become

princes and princesses and live happily ever after, the flowers are destined only for a brief moment of glory, then they wither and mix with the anonymous dust of the city. Therefore, Maria Vittoria – and especially her mother – were determined to exploit to the full extent that fleeting moment of ephemeral glory that beauty gave.

Bologna is, in fact, a small provincial city and, as such, has only one or two real elite prestigious schools. One such high school bears the name of a great scientist and is set in a building packed full of history; along its corridors have passed famous singers, ex-prime ministers and also several less illustrious alumni like your godmother!

It is an institution that you get into through tradition or by ambition. In Jasmina's case it was the calling card for the life that her family had always dreamt of: a daughter with a degree; perhaps a doctor! For Maria Vittoria it was the family school, but, above all, a fertile pond of descendants of "good" families to mix with.

Their parallel worlds crossed because of that great social leveller called public education. By an irony of the alphabet "the little frog" and the "flower" found themselves classmates. A caprice of destiny that both would have avoided, because at heart, they would both have been happy protected by their respective prejudices. Jasmina didn't like Maria Vittoria much, whom she saw as a spoilt fool. It annoyed Maria Vittoria that her blue blood and Gucci bags should coexist so closely with common mortals who wore second-hand clothes!

And so the two passed each other, term after term, without any sign of a friendship emerging or even mutual respect. High school years came and went and for Jasmina there were a succession of good marks and scholarships. For Maria Vittoria a whirlwind of more or less acceptable suitors and beauty contests. Then came the finals and the end of their enforced coexistence...at least the first of their enforced coexistences!

High school years were long over, vague recollections supressed in some remote corner of the memory, when the destinies of the two girls crossed again. This time in a maternity ward at St Thomas's Hospital, in London.

Both Bolognese heroines had finished up in London, so far from the city of their birth. The world has become ever smaller. Each of us is ever more nomadic, pushed by necessity or curiosity to pitch the "tent", or maybe just the sleeping bag, in different far-off corners of the world in a way and on a scale completely unthinkable even just a couple of decades ago. Indeed it is thought that in the last 50 years the average global distance travelled has gone up from 1,400 to 5,000 kilometres per person (or many times the length of Italy!).

But let's go back to our *Bolognesine* and to the strange coincidences of life that had brought them to those corridors of the hospital with walls that oozed bleach and alcohol.

Jasmina was on shifts at the hospital: a doctor in the accident and emergency department. The nurses sent in case after case: the cyclist with a cracked rib, the teenager who fell off a skateboard, the clumsy cooking lady who cut herself in the kitchen, and finally the pregnant woman with suspicious contractions. But immediately something in the clinical records of the pregnant woman, case 2031, caught the attention of doctor Jasmina. In black there was the name and surname of her classmate at school! Jasmina came slowly up to Maria Vittoria's bed, trying to reconcile the elegant, slim and sexy image of her classmate with the woman who was all stomach in front of her in an anonymous green smock. She realised it was the first time she had seen her without make-up and with her hair tied back modestly. "And even like that, she was still pretty," thought Jasmina.

The Frog and the Flower

Before Maria Vittoria – with her mind confused and frightened from the abdominal pain – there appeared a young doctor with such dark hair above that smock that was so white.

It was only when Jasmina addressed her in Italian. "Hey, classmate", that Maria Vittoria recognised her high school colleague in that clinical looking doctor.

"Good God!" exclaimed Maria Vittoria. "The world is certainly small!"

But before she could say anything else, a harsh pain in her back stopped her words in mid flow and transformed them into a shout for help.

The classmate, behind that white uniform, held out her hand and said, "Easy now, I'll deal with it."

Jasmina was a wonderful doctor and she took excellent care of her classmate, including recommending to her colleagues to treat her as a VIP. So Maria Vittoria found herself in her own bedroom rather than in the wards of six – those without private medical insurance.

At the end of her shift Jasmina came to Maria Vittoria's room. And while she was crossing the long corridor of the ward, she thought back on the irony of the day's event: That it was she, the fruit seller classmate, who was giving a helping hand to the undisputed princess of the high school. How times change!

Maria Vittoria was dozing when Jasmina entered the room, but awoke with a smile as soon as she felt Jasmina's hand on hers.

"Better?" Jasmina began.

Maria Vittoria – almost in tears – replied, "Thank you, thank you for everything." And added straight away, "Congratulations! You achieved your dream of being a doctor, well done!" And she said it with a deep and sincere admiration that surprised Jasmina, who remembered how the princess had such little consideration for academic success in school days.

"Congratulations to you," replied Jasmina. "You will be the mum of a beautiful baby girl who's growing healthily in your big tum."

A tear full of sweetness and tenderness streaked the pretty face of Maria Vittoria. "Yes, I hope she's strong, because I've no idea what future awaits her." And as she uttered these words, a torrent of tears overwhelmed her cheeks.

"Come on, come on," Jasmina exhorted, gripping her hand strongly.

"I am on my own," replied Maria Vittoria. "I moved here to London, two years ago, to marry a self-proclaimed prince who promised me the moon, and, as soon as I told him I was pregnant, he showed me the door, telling me he didn't know what to do with an overweight woman with potential whimpering brats!"

"Nice guy!" Jasmina said ironically.

"What little money I have put aside," continued Maria Vittoria, "won't last long. It's the truth, and I can't do anything. I always thought my beauty would be my life annuity and, indeed here I am, essentially without a penny, with only memories as an asset. My figure has vanished under six kilos of tummy – pregnant!" And Maria Vittoria's word finished with a forced smile hiding her worries.

"You're still pretty even with a tummy," Jasmina said laughing. "I've always envied the fact that you were so pretty!"

Maria Vittoria retorted, "Not much to envy…seeing how I've finished up!"

And both exploded in a deep and sincere guffaw of laughter.

After a few days, Maria Vittoria left hospital and went back "home": a bedsit in a residential area outside London, all very modest, apart from the rent which – like a lot of other things in London – had costs that were sky-high.

One Sunday when she wasn't working, Jasmina went round to see her. She rang the bell with a bunch of flowers and chocolate.

"What a nice surprise!" Maria Vittoria said immediately. "Welcome to my mini castle."

"Where did you live with your husband?" asked Jasmina.

"South Kensington, a gigantic penthouse, past times, a past life," replied Maria Vittoria, raising her eyes to the ceiling.

Jasmina, who had little time for injustices and for people who neglect their responsibilities, raged. "But why don't you ask this guy for maintenance? After all he is the father of the child. Whether he likes it or not, he has responsibilities by law."

Maria Vittoria gave a long sigh. "I know, I have tried; I've been to his house, about a week ago. The new 'me' welcomed me, tall, blond, 10 years younger and with 20 kilos less fat than me! He said to me, in no uncertain terms, that he preferred to spend money keeping his new princess."

Jasmina was about to let out a swear word as he deserved, but restraining herself, said "What he prefers is irrelevant; the law states that he has to maintain his daughter."

"That's true, but it doesn't solve my problems in practice," retorted Maria Vittoria. "Going through legal channels is expensive and takes months if not years. What can I do in the meantime?"

Just then Jasmina remembered a story that her father had told her when she was a child. It was the story of a courageous boy from Bangladesh who had escaped to Europe in search of a future better than the certain poverty that awaited him at home. He had worked hard non-stop, for four months, in the fields, but when it came to payday the employer told him, "Nada, there's no money."

The young Bangladeshi wasn't to be beaten. "I've worked and you don't pay me? It's not right and it's not legal."

At these words, it seems that the employer replied that, since the youngster was not even legally in the country, he didn't have rights and certainly couldn't go to the police, because he would have been deported straight away.

But the youngster, who had suffered pain and vexations to get to that corner of Europe in the middle of nowhere, was certainly not intimidated by the first little bully who reckoned himself smarter than he really was. And so he threatened the little bully that he would plaster the walls of that small town with information about the nasty man of the neighbourhood, revealing his faults to one and all. The little problem of not paying and other assorted weaknesses. The threat of public embarrassment prompted the little bully to review his position and to pay his dues to the young Bangladeshi.

This story inspired Jasmina who, with the enthusiasm of one who knows a thing or two, exclaimed, "There's an alternative!"

And she sounded so sure of herself that Maria Vittoria was convinced that her classmate must have had a great idea, without even having to ask what it was about.

The following day, Maria Vittoria and Jasmina went round to that nasty piece of work of her ex-boyfriend. To welcome them, they found a new "Maria Vittoria": a fusiform Barbie with an indefinable accent, bionic breasts and infinitely long legs.

The "Barbie" looked with disgust at the two *Bolognesine* and thought how many sweets they must have eaten to get like that! Immediately she said to them, "My boyfriend is busy; come back another time, in fact never!"

And saying that, she was about to close the door on them when Jasmina stuck her umbrella jamming the door and preventing it from closing.

Thereupon the "Barbie" showed that as well as being a floozy she was a complete racist. "You gipsy beggar, how dare you!"

At that insult, Maria Vittoria hit the roof even more. "To tell you the truth, my friend is Italian, of Bangladeshi origins, but I don't expect you can identify on a map where any of these nations are."

The scuffle at the door managed to distract the little bully top manager from the most important thing he was struggling with (such as choosing which Hermes tie to wear that day). He was a short guy with an arrogant manner that immediately confirmed what a nasty piece of work he clearly was. "What are you doing here? I've already told you I don't want anything to do with you and with that *thing* you've got in your stomach."

Maria Vittoria, with an icy calm, replied, "Well this *thing* – as you call her – shares your DNA (let's hope not much) and you have obligations of maintenance."

"I've got better things to do with my money; Pretty girl here," he continued, embracing the 'Barbie', "has expensive tastes."

Maria Vittoria retorted promptly, "She definitely has expensive taste, but not good taste, if she's with you. Anyhow, let's get to the point. Surprise, surprise: this conversation has all been recorded on a webcam." and thus saying, she pointed out the webcams disguised as medallions that were pinned onto their shirts. "And so, just as you don't feel you have obligations of maintenance, I don't feel much obligation to silence online. So I can't guarantee that this conversation won't go onto the internet and maybe finish up on the screens of the computers of your bosses."

The face of the little bully top manager went as white as a zombie. He immediately realised how a video with these contents in circulation could damage his career. It doesn't suit big multinational companies to have certain negative publicity and they don't like being in the news over the stupid behaviour of their employees! In reaction, the little bully lost his temper with "Barbie". "Stupid floozy! Why did you let them in?"

However, the little bully, who was arrogant, but not totally stupid, understood instantly that it was time to get out his wallet and he went into his studio, from where he came out, with a big cheque to celebrate a welcoming of the birth.

With the cheque, the two *Bolognesine* went out with their heads held high. On her way out Maria Vittoria recommended to the floozy the diet "whatever doesn't kill you makes you stronger" advised by the dietician a few years ago, telling her, "You need it, because with him, if you put on one gram of fat, you're out of work!"

When the door of that penthouse in South Kensington closed behind them, a new, happier chapter opened in Maria Vittoria's life. Three months later, Emma was born, a healthy baby, of three and a half kilos!

Since then a few years have passed. Today Emma also has a lovely little sister that Maria Vittoria has called Jasmina, in honour of the school friend who helped her in a time of need. Maria Vittoria has also found her *Prince Charming.* His name is Prince N.A.B of an old tribe in Ghana. Despite his royal lineage, Prince N.A.B works as a buyer for a supermarket chain. His castle is a small double-bedroomed flat in South London, his throne is the living room sofa from which he connects with his thousand subjects, via Skype, to administer his royal duties.

While the union of Maria Vittoria with Prince N.A.B was at first a major shock for the provincial and obtuse mind of Maria Vittoria's mother, she eventually had to accept that this prince without a castle and money was able to make her daughter much much happier than she could ever dream of for her. Of course, deep inside she still hopes that her daughter's husband may one day discover blood links with more "conventional" royal families such as the Windsors, but she is basically too busy playing with her grandchildren to worry about such trivial matters!

As for the floozy and the little bully, the financial crisis of 2008 took care of them. The little bully top manager was sacked and a little bully without fresh and plentiful banknotes is of little interest to floozies with expensive tastes. It is said, but it's not confirmed, that the trauma of the loss of the banknotes and the floozy have brought about a rapid change in his taste in women. It seems the little bully is now only interested in strictly rounded ladies.

D&D The Oaks of the Far West

Imagine an enormous stadium with big powerful lamps lighting up the sky by day like a million stars; imagine hours of queues. No, it's not a football match. The pitch is full of doctors and nurses with improvised first-aid stations, like a war zone. And no, we're not in a developing country in Africa or the Middle East, or in eighteenth century England, but in Los Angeles, in the rich United States of America in the year 2010.

This is no natural disaster. It's a day like any other in a country with many people without medical insurance. No or limited medical insurance means few or no doctors, little or no care even if you need it.

As it is a common problem in many countries, to give a hand to those in need, charitable associations like RAM® organise proper field hospitals to give medical assistance to the many who cannot afford it, using stadiums and volunteer staff from all over the world to save and improve lives that the health system may leave at risk.

And it is in one of these events organised in Los Angeles, on a hot day in April, that we meet Dan and Denise in the queue for paediatric care: two twins, known affectionately to their friends as D & D.

Their mum, Loraine, is with them, a teacher who has lost her job, and with her job the medical insurance went too. Now she works part-time; the money pays the mortgage and puts food on the table, but it's not enough to pay the cost of good medical insurance.

After several hours of queuing, D & D find themselves before an Asian female doctor, with long black hair, speaking with an unfamiliar accent. Children – thank goodness – have a curiosity without reserve, unintimidated by the formalisms of "political correctness".

D & D asked this exotic female doctor her name and where she came from. She patiently replied that her name was Jasmina; her family was from Bangladesh, but she grew up both in Italy and England.

"Bangladesh, Italy, England?" the children thought perplexedly. "Whatever is she talking about?"

Mum Loraine understood straight away that her kids were lost in that complicated world tour and said, "Tonight I'll show you these countries on Google Earth!"

D & D were healthy kids on the whole, apart from a problem they shared with many other children across America and elsewhere in the world: obesity. In other words, they were children with a few too many sweets in their belly! It is thought that a third of children in the USA are overweight, a condition that can cause them serious health problems, such as diabetes, later in life.

Jasmina examined them thoroughly and said to the mum, "Lovely children, but they need a bit of dieting so they grow as strong as an oak; otherwise they risk just becoming little bushes with little protection from the winds of illness."

At these words, D & D said in chorus, "We want to be an oak!" And everyone laughed happily.

D & D had been so good in the long wait at the stadium

hospital that, in the evening, Loraine rewarded them by taking them to the play area in the park: a go on the see-saw, a couple of turns on the slide, and a few rolls in the sand. Sue was at the park too – another mother with two children. Sue was also a single mother with a part-time job, with (too) many bills to pay and too little in her purse.

Sue and Loraine often fantasised about how nice it would be to be able to afford a few extra luxuries: like a monthly manicure or a new dress, but more than anything else they dreamt of not having to worry about their mortgage payments or the cost of sending the kids to school and medical expenses.

That evening in the park, Loraine confided in Sue about her fears for the children's obesity. "Healthy food and organic produce cost a lot – definitely outside the budget of a mum with a part-time job," Loraine lamented. "And children really don't like so-called healthy foods – they have quite a different palate!"

Sue, whose children suffered the same problem, nodded and fully agreed with her friend. And while she was thinking this, Denise got stuck in the slide. She was just too chubby to slide down easily. Sadly, all the children around started to laugh maliciously and poor Denise felt mortified and burst into tears.

Loraine got up from the bench with a feline leap to remove her little cub from the laughter of her peers. She picked her up by her arms and led her away from the cruel laughter.

Having dried Denise's tears away from her face, Loraine took her kids and went home. The children were safe in their little beds with their blankets covered in orange stars, lights out, silence everywhere. But Loraine couldn't sleep. The image of her child humiliated and isolated because of her weight tormented her like a weight on her heart. She wondered how many other similar cruelties lay ahead for her children, not to mention potential health problems. And in the torment of these dark thoughts, she swore to herself she would find a solution.

A woman who fights for her kids is a force of nature stronger and more indomitable than a volcano that reawakens after a thousand years!

So, in the name of motherly love, Loraine shut herself in the library of the school where she worked day after day with just one mission: how to cook food that was acceptable to the palate and the figure! She read books on biology, physiology and psychology and every other "ology" you can imagine.

Her studies, in which she carried out experiments, brought mixed success. But in the end the efforts paid off and she managed to put together a menu that the health and playfulness of the kids demanded.

Soon enough, Sue and a couple of other mums in the neighbourhood who had children with "sweet round cheeks" united with Loraine's efforts and they too started to contribute recipes to the menu "children strong and healthy as an oak". They created green biscuits with clowns' faces: a lot of mint, few calories and a smile assured. Another great success was the multi-coloured spaghetti that looked like a rainbow on the plate.

The recipes were often born late at night when the mums, having put the kids to bed, met in one another's kitchens to play at being chefs. They shared recipes and gossip, all garnished with a lot of laughter!

And the efforts of these mums, in time, started to bear good fruit, with the kids visibly losing weight and their faces literally pictures of health.

And given that good news travels fast, Loraine and the other mums of the "children strong and healthy as an oak" operation acquired a certain notoriety in the district. Many other mums started to approach the mums of the "oak" for advice or even just to pay them compliments.

Such was the success of this healthy food club that one day Loraine and Sue had the idea of trying to start a small business – a small weekend stall for selling food healthy as an oak. They were something like a thousand dollars short of investment; however, neither Sue nor Loraine had that amount of savings.

Small entrepreneurs, that are often the lifeblood of the economy and of innovation, may find the first steps quite challenging; among them, one can often find rare gems such as Steve Jobs, the man who created the iPad you play with so much, or Walt Disney, the father of the animated cartoons that you devour, my dear godchildren.

And the first entrepreneurial steps Sue and Loraine took met with plenty of nos and frustration typical of those same small entrepreneurs in search of that first loan to start their business. The objections were many and clichéd: "you are teachers, not business people; you have no capital of your own...blah blah blah!"

But as we said before, a mum fighting for her children is a force of nature that is impossible to contain. In the end it was that modern miracle called the internet that gave a hand to the mums of Los Angeles. In their nightly studies into how to finance their lines of healthy but succulent foods, Sue and Loraine became aware of an innovative concept called "crowdfunding", in other words small private investors interested in giving a hand to (for now) small entrepreneurs without the brokering of third parties.

Crowdfunding is a bit like "once upon a time there was the village credit", when people invested their own savings in businesses or in individuals mostly by direct acquaintance, based on personal faith and an often intuitive evaluation of the project, without the brokering of the conventional banking system or other third parties. The only difference is that then the acquaintance was at a personal level: members of the same village, parishioners, relatives... Today it is about virtual communities where small entrepreneurs from the Great Rift Valley in Kenya, Mexico City or LA have a direct line to investors from New York to Hong Kong and vice-versa. For the giant numbers of world finance, the volumes associated with crowdfunding are like a drop in the ocean, but even a drop can make a difference to those who are thirsty for water.

The idea of healthy foods to bring up children strong as an oak soon intrigued several members of the global investment community. And so Rosy, a mum from the Mid-West, invested 20 dollars, followed by Colette, a woman permanently on a diet from Milton Keynes in England, and they were joined by a pair of friends from the local Weight Watchers club...

And so, click after click, Sue and Loraine found themselves with the 2,000 dollars of capital they needed and as many as 50 investors including housewives, dieters and also a certain Hope, a Kenyan airline trainee-pilot.

And for Sue and Loraine that drop of capital opened up a sea of opportunities. They hired a van and started to distribute their products at local fairs and street markets. Quite soon they were able to cover the cost of the van and took on a person full-time to sell at the markets. With a full-time person and a van available the "Oak" could spread its roots, and the cottage industry began to transform itself into a permanent presence in all the best farmer's markets in Los Angeles.

And since excess roundness is a problem that strikes all postcodes and social classes, the idea of little clown-effect low calorie biscuits quite soon found many fans. For example, they caught the attention of Messrs. V & M, great enthusiasts of farmer's markets, good food and – like a lot of people – with a few too many extra pounds! They bought a packet that ended up at a dinner of other foodies and there wasn't a single one left.

The foodie friends of V & M began to ask for the Oak biscuits from the supermarkets in the "well off" areas and they started to talk about them with their suppliers. And so, by word of mouth and a certain amount of luck, the community of fans of the Oak grew. In the course of just a year, the Oak even managed to get its roots into the high distribution supermarkets.

Today the Oak and its little green clown-effect biscuits is a healthy and profitable business and gives work (and medical insurance) to many mums and dads.

D & D, our oaks of the Far West, grow healthy and beautiful in perfect shape! Sue and Loraine can now afford the not inconsiderable luxury of medical insurance, manicures and chic dresses.

Rosy, Colette, Hope and the other virtual investors of the crowdfunding venture also smile because they have more than doubled the initial value of their investment... a smile as healthy and strong as an oak!

Ming Ming's Merry Go Round

Close your eyes, dear godchildren. Imagine a squad of blue uniformed men on bicycles; low-built houses; dusty roads full of holes; no advertising billboards; the horizon breached by the sky interrupted from time to time by images of Mao, the father of modern China: proud, his eyes fixed on the future, behind him the flapping red of the Chinese flag.

Underneath one of these giant posters Ming-ming, a lively Chinese child with disobedient pigtails, was sitting. She was squatting with a bowl full of rice made by a grandmother with hair as white as a seagull.

Twenty years have passed since that day. No more blue uniforms and the Peking of low-built houses. Today in Beijing it's much easier to see Armani and Calvin Klein suits at the wheel of powerful cars speeding between urban forest of glass and metal skyscrapers that seem to touch the clouds.

And the little Ming-ming? A modern hairstyle has taken the place of the disobedient pigtails. She has a cigarette in her hand (terrible habit!) instead of a bowl of rice. She is standing looking at those enormous skyscrapers and, in their anonymous greyness, she is searching for the bushes and characteristics of the district where she had been a child.

49

Many years had passed since that night when her parents wrapped Ming-ming up in the only blanket they had and, armed with a sheet full of their few possessions and a thousand hopes, they ventured out into the dark night.

Of that journey Ming-ming remembers interminable marches in the wilderness, the bitter taste of hunger and cold that freezes you inside. But above all she remembers the sea, the first time she had seen it: so immense and blue.

After weeks of walking and struggles, Ming-ming and her parents had arrived at the port of Shanghai: an anthill of boats large and small. Even today when Ming-ming thinks of the sea, that smell of rotting fish and kerosene fills her head immediately.

At that time you needed strict permission to go from one city to another in China. This was a luxury granted to few so Ming-ming and her family were travelling illegally. Then in Shanghai they played hide-and-seek with the police who otherwise would have asked them for personal documentation which they did not have and without them Ming-ming and her family would have been returned home or at worse imprisoned. To hide from the police, Ming-ming and her parents pulled out all the stops. They made themselves tiny to squeeze into battered boxes. Once they even threw themselves into the rubbish.

Ming-ming doesn't remember if that playing hide-and-seek lasted days or weeks or even longer... every day blurred into the next, indistinguishable in that life of struggles and fear.

Then one fine day, Ming-ming and her family set sail on a dilapidated boat. As quick as a flash they got on board at dead of night.

Packed tightly with other hopeful travellers, they abandoned themselves to the mercy of those infinite waters aboard a floating wreck. The waters of the ocean were rough and icy, sometimes with waves as big as a house beating against the boat. Even if she was protected by the strong embrace of her parents, Ming-ming was afraid of those waters as fierce as dragons: they made the wreck that carried her dance violently. She and her parents and scores of other hopeful travellers were voyaging towards a future that they hoped would be rosier than the gloomy past they were leaving behind.

There are many reasons for leaving. Some – like your godmother – can afford the luxury of travelling for curiosity, but many do so out of necessity. Necessity of survival, to give themselves and their families the chance of a life worthy of the name.

Ming-ming and her family were heading for Australia, or so they thought. But that wreck, which unscrupulous men dared to call a ship, didn't have the makings (or more precisely the steel) to navigate the oceans and land on the wild coasts of Australia.

Days after departure, the wreck was swamped by the most powerful of waves which at a stroke capsized that piece of battered raft and swept all its passengers into the sea.

Everyone screamed as that wreck overturned on itself: some cried out for God, some their forefathers, some the names of their loved ones.

When Ming-ming thinks back to that moment, her most vivid memory is the strong embrace of her parents which protected her from the furious sea like a suit of armour.

Ming-ming's parents were young and healthy, but above all they were armed with the indomitable strength of hope. United in their embrace, they carried on swimming and sustaining each other for hours, maybe even a full day, until a ship spotted them. It was a coastguard motorboat and it appeared to them as a miraculous ray of sun in that tempestuous sea.

Exhausted by the cold, tiredness and hunger, Ming-ming and her parents were lifted onto the motorboat, together with other tormented souls miraculously saved from the fury of the sea and the negligence of unscrupulous men. Ming-ming and her parents were transported to a strange land, where tall men – with skin so white that to Ming-ming they seemed like zombies – spoke an incomprehensible language. They had arrived in Australia, or rather in a refugee camp in the north of Australia.

The camp, their deliverance from the stormy waters and from a past that didn't seem to offer a future, was in the form of an expanse of land populated by tents arranged neatly on fenced-off terrain. The camp authorities took due care of Ming-ming and her family: food, vaccinations and a hot shower (a luxury that Ming-ming wasn't used to).

They even gave them a tent all to themselves – more space than Ming-ming and her family had ever had. Although to Ming-ming the refugee camp seemed in many ways a five-star hotel, there was always that strange sensation of a world artificially enclosed behind insurmountable walls of metal.

Through the fences Ming-ming could glimpse a world of coloured cars, giant advertising billboards that – to her great surprise – did not show the face of the leader Mao, but families with objects completely unknown to her, electric lawnmowers, colour TVs and, marvel of all marvels, an inflatable pool full of floating plastic animals.

Ming-ming was fascinated by that world of which she could only steal glimpses through the wire mesh. She often asked her parents why she couldn't cross that fence. To which her parents optimistically answered, "Soon, you'll see, soon."

To get past that metal fence you needed a regular permit to stay. A piece of paper longed for by many and with it the chance to build yourself a future in that far-off land. Permits to stay are few and customarily go to people with particular professional qualifications: doctors, engineers, university professors and researchers. Ming-ming's parents were without such qualifications, but they had an absolutely unshakeable optimism.

And as they say, "God helps those who help themselves." And in this case Ming-ming's parents helped themselves a lot. They both set themselves the task of learning the local language, then they befriended the staff of the camp with a haircut, a jacket ironed, and the occasional dish of sweet-and-sour pork.

One of the doctors in the camp, a certain Doctor MCM, was touched by the case of that energetic and enterprising family. They reminded him a bit of his flight from Europe in wartime in search of a better future, many many years ago.

Doctor MCM had relatives in New Zealand: a very far-off land but a generous one by nature: great pastures, water. They were elderly people without children but with a farm to look after.

Months passed before Ming-ming's family could permanently leave the refugee camp for Otorohanga, a forgotten corner of an equally remote land.

New Zealand, a territory almost as vast as Italy, situated in the southern hemisphere of the world, near the Pole, has little more than four million inhabitants. The funny thing is there are more cows and sheep than humans!

Endless expanses of green, a long blue coastline, silent volcanoes. In the past many Chinese people emigrated to New Zealand to mine gold. They found little gold, but that fertile land produced agricultural riches that today are worth as much as gold, if not more.

Hans and Regina were two energetic farmers even in old age. Germanic stature, broad smiles, they seemed giants next to Ming-ming and her family.

They were emigrants from Germany in the 1940s who had made a long and tortuous journey by ship and on foot. Armed only with their labour, without speaking a word of English, they rolled up their sleeves and, one harvesting and pressing after another, had built a farm that then gave work to at least 10 people.

Hans and Regina recognised immediately in that lively Chinese family the same desire for a better life as the one that drove them there so many years ago, so right from the first day they cast a benevolent eye over Ming-ming and her family.

The work was hard, very hard, because cattle and the land don't have days off, but food was plentiful and Ming-ming could run and play to her heart's content in the enormous expanses of the farm.

Unfortunately the farm was rather isolated and there were no children around; sheep and cows were Ming-ming's playmates. She chased them in the meadows, playing hide-and-seek. She knew each of them by name!

Because of the distances, Ming-ming didn't go to school regularly. She was educated at home by mum, dad, Hans, Regina and the other helpers. Although everyone did whatever they could to give Ming-ming a good education, it was a gang that was more at home among cattle and corn than books so unfortunately, quite soon, even Ming-ming began to see school as a distraction from the things that really mattered in her life: rearing, the fields, cooking.

Ming-ming particularly loved the kitchen. A huge room with a wooden table that was strong and robust and a wood burning stove that could heat the entire place. That was Regina's realm and Ming-ming grew up spending hours watching the Teutonic matron making rich, calorific foods. When age began to get the better of the elderly matron, Ming-

ming happily took Regina's place as cook supreme. Regina really liked seeing the little Chinese girl at ease among the stoves making Wiener Schnitzel and Bratkartoffeln.

With Hans and Regina more tired by age every day, Ming-ming and her family were ever more occupied in running all aspects of the farm. Ming-ming soon abandoned school to dedicate herself to the farm full-time; even at a very young age she managed the sale of milk and other products with more experience than her parents.

Many years had already passed since their arrival at Otorohanga when Ming-ming's father – that man so full of optimism – became seriously ill: cancer. Against that illness that strikes millions of people around the world, optimism was not enough. In the space of a few months Ming-ming's father died like a flower after the spring.

Ming-ming and her mum decided to take her father's ashes back to China to rest next to the other ancestors. Despite considerable economic and technological changes, China remains – thank goodness – a place strongly linked to its own traditions with respect for ancestors and for the family, one of the values most rooted in the cultural DNA.

However, the trip to China was expensive and so to put some extra money aside, Ming-ming decided to go and sell milk directly door to door to the families of Otorohanga. She got up at dawn and went knocking from door to door in the suburbs of Otorohanga and with the motto "fresh milk straight from the cow's udder" she raised a smile and a sale with great ease.

The model "from the udder to the consumer" was such a success that very soon, encouraged by Hans and Regina, Ming-ming and her mum set up a mini distribution network covering the most affluent areas of Otorohanga.

In a short time, the door to door service grew and they began to open proper milk bars – fixed distribution points where people from the city could buy the freshly milked product. Ming-ming and her mum called their milk bar "M M", after the name of their first benefactor, the Doctor of the refugee camp. But the combination of the initials MM and fresh milk meant that the locals soon began to nickname their bars Mumu.

Thanks to the commercial success of Mumu, Ming-ming and her mum were finally able to take the ashes of her dad to China. Many years had passed since the start of their flight from their homeland. They had escaped almost in shame, but they were returning like heroes with great fanfares, welcomed by the family with endless celebrations.

The Peking that Ming-ming had left had low-built houses and lots of bicycles. That which she returned to had more cars and boutiques than Otorohanga. Ming-ming, now a grown woman, struggled to recognise the city of her childhood, the city of the bowls of rice with granny Xiang.

Being there gave her strange sensations. On one hand she was cheered by the sense of familiarity in being surrounded by people who speak the same language, on the other she felt a little awkward in that world that was so frenetic: she, who was used to the rhythms of the countryside, to the healthy air of the fields, struggled to adapt to the smoke of the city and the hurrying this way and that.

But most of all she missed the healthy food of the farm, especially its milk: the milk she drank every day as fresh as possible straight from the cow. China represents what can be described as a real economic miracle. From when the process of reform started in 1978, China has grown almost 10 per cent every year and today is one of the largest, if not, the largest of all.

I know that talk of 10 per cent is a bit abstract; so let me try to put a face, or rather many faces, to that otherwise anonymous number. The Chinese economic boom has created more middle-class consumers than the entire population of the USA; they sell more cars and more mobile phones than in many countries in the western world.

Today Chinese shoppers buy roughly one in four luxury goods: pretty items such as Bottega Veneta bags, displayed in windows like jewels, or precious gems by Bulgari or Cartier, bright enough to light up the night. Yes, because today there are more than a million Chinese millionaires! And the number of magnates "made in China" is destined to grow and maybe overtake Japan and the United States, that at the moment dominate the league of the super-rich.

Naturally, China also has its challenges, including pollution and, rather more important for our story, food safety.

When one talks of food, naturally the number one preoccupation is having enough of it to feed oneself. However, another important dimension is the quality of the food. Is the food good enough not to give health problems? This is a topic that many countries worry about as millions of people fall sick due to poor food quality every year (nearly six million in the UK alone and many times that in the US!).

When our Ming-ming returned to China to bring back the ashes of her father, she certainly didn't think of the subject of food safety, let alone the new class of millionaires. She certainly realised that China had changed greatly from when she ate rice, squatting under the poster of Mao with her grandmother, and there was definitely more money to go round.

However, hers was a much simpler reasoning, more of a "gut feeling" like most of the best ideas in business often are. The freshest milk, straight from the cow, produced by animals happy to gambol in the green fields is seriously good, and delicious too! And if she found it delicious, why wouldn't her compatriots?

Back in the pleasant land of New Zealand where they

carried on milking decent profits from the Mumu bars, the enterprising Ming-ming and her hard-working mum launched a new venture: "Mumu" out to conquer China!

However, China is not a market that can be conquered by thinking small, with a few provincial boutiques. China has more than a billion people, more than 150 cities with more than a million inhabitants and the 10 largest cities – most of which the majority of us wouldn't know the names of, let alone where they are on a map – have an overall population of more than 70 million people, or more than the whole of France.

Ming-ming and her mum strove hard to open the eyes of other independent milk producers to the great opportunities in China. It wasn't easy; some were prejudiced, others preferred to be big fish in small ponds rather than small fish in big ones, but in the end the enthusiasm, persuasion and tenacity of the two founders of Mumu, as well as the prospect of considerable earnings, brought about the formation of a consortium founded in New Zealand to distribute fresh milk en masse in the vast Chinese market.

And, as they say, the rest is history. A history told by Forbes and other Meccas of enterprise. Many members of the original consortium retired at an old age with more money than they thought they could ever come up with.

Even Ming-ming didn't have to worry any more about money or getting up at dawn to distribute milk. But she has no plans to give up. Mumu today is a food company synonymous with quality and interests in three continents. Recently there has been talk of an innovative company founded by courageous mums, "Food Strong as an Oak". The last time I saw Ming-ming she was in an airport: she was headed for Los Angeles, this time out to conquer the healthy food of the west.

Epilogue

Dear godchildren,

So we've reached the end of our waltz around the world.

Knowing you, curious creatures as you are, I know you'd like to know how the stories of the Green Cinderellas, Hope and the other courageous heroines of our tales ended.

Naturally, you could talk of the great commercial and personal successes they have achieved over the years; of how, for example, Hope opened one of the best pilot training schools in the world.

But the really important thing is that their stories – like those of many people who, thank God, have the courage to follow their dreams – in reality never end. Their dreams are the lifeblood that allows other dreams to be born and multiply.

Dreams have no limits; dreams see opportunities where others see only problems. Our dreams are the secret weapon that humanity has to create an ever better world.

In our waltz around the world we have talked about many complex problems and how the tenacity, audacity and optimism of our heroines and of their equally formidable accomplices have helped resolve them.

When you have as many grey hairs as your godmother (alas!), many of the problems we've talked about – obesity, excess waste, access to medical care – will perhaps be just a distant memory, resolved with methods unimaginable now, created by brilliant dreamers.

Fortunately, in my waltz around the world, I have met many dreamers: some brilliant, others not; some with big dreams, others small. But they all had something in common: the rejection of artificial and stupid limits, imposed by "fear-o-saurs".

Fear-o-saurs are the antithesis of dreamers: they oppose every kind of change, they hide behind absurd barriers that in time surrender to dreams like paper banks on a river in full flow.

Fear-o-saurs infest all social levels and every corner of the world; and often they are the number one obstacle to resolving the problems of a planet of seven billion people.

Unfortunately, sooner or later, you too will meet your fear-o-saurs and their absurd rules and barriers erected with the sole purpose of justifying and feeding their fears; this will cause you frustration and acid indigestion. But don't you worry because the person who dreams always triumphs over the fear-o-saurs.

The first piece of advice – to tell the truth, the only one in this pocket guide to this complicated world full of opportunities – is this: let the force of your dreams crush the fear-o-saurs and their limits, so you'll write the most beautiful story for your life and for others!